Dr. Barbara Herbal Tea Bible

100+ Herbal Tea Recipes Inspired by Barbara O'Neill's
Teachings | Powerful Blends for Holistic Healing and Greater
Well-Being

Jacqueline Bridge

Table of Contents

Cold and Flu Relief

INTRODUCTION

Welcome to a journey that transcends the mere act of sipping tea, venturing deep into the heart of wellness, tradition, and the natural world. Inspired by the teachings of Barbara O'Neill, this herbal tea cookbook is more than a collection of recipes; it is an invitation to explore the ancient wisdom and modern science behind herbal remedies. Each page, each recipe, is a step towards understanding how the simple act of brewing tea can be transformed into a powerful ritual for health, healing, and harmony. In these pages, you'll discover not just the art of tea making but the art of living well. From the lush fields of green tea to the aromatic gardens of chamomile and lavender, from the robust depths of dandelion roots to the delicate whispers of elderflower, this book is a testament to the earth's bounty and its capacity to nourish and heal. It's a homage to the time-honored traditions that have revered nature as the ultimate healer, bringing to light the interconnectedness of body, mind, and spirit.

As you turn each page, you'll embark on a voyage through history and culture, exploring the role of tea in societies around the globe and its evolution as a beacon of health and wellness. You'll delve into the healing power of various tea types, understanding how green, black, herbal, and beyond can offer unique benefits, from boosting immunity and enhancing energy to supporting digestion and soothing the soul. But this book is not merely about observation; it's about action. It's a guide to crafting your herbal tea remedies, a hands-on manual that empowers you to blend, brew, and savor teas that resonate with your health needs and wellness goals. It's about harnessing the potency of herbs, mastering brewing techniques, and navigating the nuances of herbal safety and interactions, ensuring that every cup you craft is a step towards optimal health. So, whether you're a seasoned tea enthusiast or new to the world of herbal brews, this cookbook offers you the keys to unlocking the full spectrum of natural healing. It invites you to pour, sip, and revel in the profound connection between the herbal cup and the heart, embarking on a transformative journey towards wellness, one tea leaf at a time.

Yours in health and happiness,

Jacqueline Bridge

THE ROLE OF TEA IN NATURAL HEALTH

Tea, the second most consumed beverage in the world after water, transcends mere culinary delight, embedding itself deeply within the tapestry of societies and emerging as a potent healing elixir. Its journey from ancient ritual to modern-day health staple reflects a confluence of cultural traditions, historical significance, and scientific research, underscoring tea's integral role in natural health practices. This chapter delves into the historical and cultural significance of tea as a healing beverage and elucidates how different types of teas—green, black, herbal, and others—offer a spectrum of health benefits.

Historical and Cultural Significance

The tapestry of tea's history is a rich and colorful narrative, interwoven with myths, traditions, and a profound reverence for nature. Its origins, rooted in ancient legend, speak of a fortuitous blend of fate and herbal mastery. The story begins with the Chinese Emperor Shen Nong, a figure revered not only as a ruler but also as a pioneering herbalist, whose curiosity about the natural world forever changed human consumption of beverages.

In the year 2737 BC, as the tale unfolds, Shen Nong was purifying water by boiling it beneath the shade of a wild tea tree. By a whisper of fate, leaves from the tree were caught by the wind, cascading into his pot and imparting a delicate hue and an enticing aroma to the water. This accidental infusion revealed the tea leaf's transformative power, marking the birth of tea as a healing elixir. This serendipitous discovery was more than just the birth of a beverage; it was the inception of tea's enduring legacy as a cornerstone of Chinese culture and medicine. Tea's medicinal virtues, once unveiled, became a beacon of health, embedding itself deeply within the ethos of Chinese society. It was celebrated not only for its delightful flavor but for its profound ability to harmonize the body and mind, aid digestion, and invigorate the spirit. As tea's renown spread, it wove itself into the fabric of daily life, becoming synonymous with wellness and tranquility.

The allure of tea transcended the borders of China, making its way along the Silk Road and across the seas, sowing seeds of tradition in every land it touched. In Japan, the introduction of tea gave rise to the "Chanoyu" or Japanese tea ceremony, an intricate ritual that transcends the act of drinking tea to embody a philosophy of harmony, respect, purity, and tranquility. This ceremonial practice elevates the preparation and consumption of tea to a spiritual act, reflecting the deep integration of tea into the cultural and spiritual life of Japan.

In India, tea found a different expression. It became woven into the Ayurvedic tradition, where it was enhanced with a variety of herbs and spices, creating an array of healing brews. Each blend was tailored to balance the body's doshas—vata, pitta, and kapha—demonstrating the versatility of tea as a medicinal agent capable of restoring health and vitality. The journey of tea to the West marked a new chapter in its storied history. By the 16th century, tea had reached Europe, where it quickly became a symbol of sophistication and social status. In England, the tradition of afternoon tea emerged as a quintessential social ritual, albeit with a lesser emphasis on the medicinal properties that had defined tea's role in Eastern cultures. Yet, even as the context changed, the intrinsic appeal of tea—its ability to soothe, uplift, and connect—remained a constant.

Across these diverse cultures, tea has been revered not just as a beverage but as a powerful symbol of healing, community, and harmony with nature. Its story is a testament to the universal human desire for balance and well-being, and its enduring popularity underscores tea's role as a timeless elixir of health. From the ancient hills of China to the modern tea rooms of the world, tea continues to be a source of comfort and rejuvenation, a bridge between the past and present, and a shared cup of wellness for humanity.

The Healing Power of Different Tea Types

The world of tea offers a treasure trove of health benefits, each type boasting its unique blend of healing properties. From the verdant fields where these teas are harvested to the steaming cups in which they are served, the journey of tea is a testament to its potent medicinal qualities.

Green Tea: With its verdant hue and delicate flavor, stands as a pillar in the temple of natural health. Its minimal processing ensures that the leaves retain a maximum concentration of antioxidants, particularly catechins like epigallocatechin gallate (EGCG). This potent compound is a vanguard against oxidative stress, offering protection at the cellular level against chronic diseases. Studies illuminate green tea's multifaceted role in enhancing cardiovascular health, championing it as a guardian of the heart. Its influence extends to the realm of weight management, where it accelerates metabolism and fat oxidation, and its protective aura may even extend to reducing the risk of certain cancers. Moreover, green tea is a beacon of hope in the fight against cognitive decline, offering a shield against the shadows of neurodegenerative diseases, thus securing its revered status in the pantheon of health-enhancing beverages.

Black Tea: With its bold flavors and deeper oxidation, carves its own niche in health lore. It's a tapestry woven with theaflavins and thearubigins, antioxidants that dance in harmony to support heart health and lower cholesterol levels. This tea's rich profile has been linked to a harmonious blood pressure and a reduced risk of stroke, painting it as a stalwart ally in cardiovascular wellness. Additionally, the judicious caffeine content in black tea acts as a clarion call to mental alertness, cutting through the fog of fatigue and potentially guarding against the onset of type 2 diabetes. Thus, black tea serves not just as a comforting beverage but as a robust protector of holistic health.

Herbal Teas: Herbal teas, or tisanes, are the wild gardens of the tea world, offering a cornucopia of health benefits that vary as widely as their ingredients. From the serene embrace of chamomile, easing us into restful slumber and aiding digestion, to the invigorating touch of peppermint, offering solace from digestive turmoil and headaches, each herb sings its own healing aria. Echinacea stands tall as a sentinel of immunity, while the vibrant hibiscus flower, with its tart charm, acts as a natural tonic for blood pressure. Rooibos, with its antioxidant prowess, weaves a protective spell for the heart and wards off the specters of cancer. This diverse ensemble of herbal teas offers a symphony of natural remedies, addressing a plethora of health concerns with each soothing sip.

Oolong Tea: Wwith its enigmatic character—poised between the green freshness and the rich oxidation of black tea—offers a bouquet of health benefits. Celebrated for its role in weight management, oolong tea is a muse for metabolism, encouraging the body to burn fat more efficiently.

Its contributions to heart health and skin vitality paint it as a versatile elixir, while its potential in regulating blood sugar levels casts it as a guardian of glycemic balance. Oolong tea, with its nuanced flavors and health benefits, is a testament to the art of tea processing and its impact on wellness.

White Tea: White tea, the most delicate of teas, is a whisper of the tea leaf's natural state, offering a treasure trove of antioxidants in their most pristine form. Its minimal processing preserves a purity that is protective against heart disease and the ravages of cancer. White tea's gentle embrace extends to the skin, shielding it from the aging effects of oxidative stress and preserving the vitality of youth. It is a tea of subtle strength, offering a quiet but potent defense against the trials of time and disease.

Tea's journey from a simple leaf to a globally cherished beverage underscores its profound cultural and historical significance. Beyond its role in social rituals, tea has carved a niche in the domain of natural health, offering a diverse palette of flavors and health benefits. The rich tapestry of green, black, herbal, oolong, and white teas presents a holistic approach to wellness, emphasizing prevention, healing, and balance. As modern science continues to uncover the health secrets of tea, this ancient beverage remains a testament to nature's capacity to nurture and heal. The story of tea, interwoven with strands of history, culture, and science, continues to evolve, reminding us of the simple yet profound joys and benefits found in a cup of tea.

HERBAL TEAS & THEIR PROPERTIES

Herbal teas, or tisanes, have been cherished across cultures and epochs not merely as beverages of leisure but as potent vessels of healing and wellness. Unlike traditional teas derived from the Camellia sinensis plant, herbal teas are brewed from a diverse palette of herbs, spices, flowers, and fruits, each bringing its unique medicinal properties to the cup. This chapter delves into the verdant world of herbal teas, exploring the health benefits of common herbs and how these delightful infusions can be used to treat specific conditions or enhance overall wellness.

The Herbal Pantry: Common Herbs and Their Benefits

1. Chamomile (Matricaria recutita)

Benefits: Promotes relaxation, aids sleep, reduces stress, soothes stomach aches, and mitigates menstrual cramps.

Conditions Treated: Insomnia, anxiety, digestive discomfort, PMS.

2. Peppermint (Mentha piperita)

Benefits: Enhances digestion, relieves headaches, reduces bloating, and soothes irritable bowel syndrome (IBS) symptoms.

Conditions Treated: Digestive issues, migraines, IBS.

3. Ginger (Zingiber officinale)

Benefits: Combats nausea, stimulates digestion, reduces inflammation, and supports immune function.

Conditions Treated: Morning sickness, motion sickness, arthritis, colds, and flu.

4. Hibiscus (Hibiscus sabdariffa)

Benefits: Lowers blood pressure, supports liver health, contains antioxidants, and may aid in weight loss.

Conditions Treated: Hypertension, liver disorders, metabolic syndrome.

5. Echinacea (Echinacea spp.)

Benefits: Boosts the immune system, fights infections, and reduces cold and flu duration.

Conditions Treated: Common cold, upper respiratory infections.

6. Rooibos (Aspalathus linearis)

Benefits: Rich in antioxidants, promotes heart health, and may reduce cancer risk.

Conditions Treated: Cardiovascular disease prevention, oxidative stress.

7. Lavender (Lavandula angustifolia)

Benefits: Promotes relaxation and sleep, reduces anxiety, and has anti-inflammatory properties.

Conditions Treated: Anxiety, insomnia, stress-related conditions.

8. Lemon Balm (Melissa officinalis)

Benefits: Enhances mood, supports cognitive function, aids digestion, and promotes calmness.

Conditions Treated: Anxiety, cognitive impairment, digestive issues.

9. Dandelion (Taraxacum officinale)

Benefits: Supports liver detoxification, promotes digestion, and acts as a diuretic.

Conditions Treated: Liver ailments, bloating, digestive disorders.

10. Nettle (Urtica dioica)

Benefits: Rich in nutrients, supports joint health, aids in allergy relief, and promotes urinary tract health.

Conditions Treated: Arthritis, seasonal allergies, urinary conditions.

11. Yarrow (Achillea millefolium)

Benefits: Supports wound healing, reduces fever, aids in digestion, and can relieve menstrual cramps.

Conditions Treated: Colds, fevers, gastrointestinal discomfort, menstrual pain.

12. Milk Thistle (Silybum marianum)

Benefits: Promotes liver health, supports detoxification, and may protect against liver diseases.

Conditions Treated: Liver disorders, gallbladder issues, detoxification.

13. Valerian Root (Valeriana officinalis)

Benefits: Aids sleep, reduces anxiety, and can alleviate stress.

Conditions Treated: Insomnia, anxiety, stress-related disorders.

14. Fennel (Foeniculum vulgare)

Benefits: Enhances digestion, relieves bloating, and can ease menstrual cramps.

Conditions Treated: Digestive discomfort, IBS, menstrual pain.

15. Licorice Root (Glycyrrhiza glabra)

Benefits: Soothes gastrointestinal problems, relieves respiratory ailments, and supports adrenal function.

Conditions Treated: Stomach ulcers, bronchitis, adrenal insufficiency.

16. Sage (Salvia officinalis)

Benefits: Enhances cognitive function, supports throat health, and has antioxidant properties.

Conditions Treated: Sore throats, cognitive decline, oxidative stress.

17. Spearmint (Mentha spicata)

Benefits: Aids digestion, relieves nausea, and can improve hormonal balance.

Conditions Treated: Digestive issues, nausea, hormonal disorders.

18. Thyme (Thymus vulgaris)

Benefits: Has antimicrobial properties, supports respiratory health, and boosts immunity.

Conditions Treated: Coughs, bronchitis, immune support.

19. Ashwagandha (Withania somnifera)

Benefits: Reduces stress and anxiety, improves energy levels, and supports overall wellness.

Conditions Treated: Stress, fatigue, general wellness.

20. Holy Basil (Ocimum sanctum)

Benefits: Reduces stress, lowers blood sugar levels, and has anti-inflammatory properties.

Conditions Treated: Stress, diabetes, inflammation.

21. Cinnamon (Cinnamomum verum)

Benefits: Regulates blood sugar, has antioxidant properties, and supports digestive health.

Conditions Treated: Diabetes, digestive discomfort, oxidative stress.

22. Goldenseal (Hydrastis canadensis)

Benefits: Has antimicrobial and anti-inflammatory properties, supports mucous membrane health.

Conditions Treated: Colds, flu, digestive infections.

23. Cardamom (Elettaria cardamomum)

Benefits: Aids digestion, relieves nausea, and has detoxifying effects.

Conditions Treated: Digestive issues, detoxification.

24. Clove (Syzygium aromaticum)

Benefits: Relieves dental pain, has antiseptic properties, and supports digestion.

Conditions Treated: Toothache, indigestion, microbial infections.

25. Calendula (Calendula officinalis)

Benefits: Promotes skin healing, has anti-inflammatory properties, and supports lymphatic health.

Conditions Treated: Skin irritations, inflammation, lymphatic congestion.

26. Marshmallow Root (Althaea officinalis)

Benefits: Soothes mucous membranes, aids in respiratory and digestive health.

Conditions Treated: Sore throat, cough, digestive irritation.

27. Passionflower (Passiflora incarnata)

Benefits: Promotes relaxation, aids sleep, and reduces anxiety.

Conditions Treated: Insomnia, anxiety, stress.

28. St. John's Wort (Hypericum perforatum)

Benefits: Alleviates mild to moderate depression, reduces anxiety, and has anti-inflammatory properties.

Conditions Treated: Depression, anxiety, nerve pain.

29. Rosemary (Rosmarinus officinalis)

Benefits: Enhances memory and concentration, supports liver and digestive health.

Conditions Treated: Cognitive function, digestive issues, liver support.

30. Burdock Root (Arctium lappa)

Benefits: Detoxifies the blood, supports skin health, and aids in digestion.

Conditions Treated: Skin conditions, digestive issues, detoxification.

Crafting Your Herbal Tea Remedies

Crafting the perfect herbal tea remedy is an art form that marries tradition with personal wellness. It's a process that demands mindfulness, respect for nature, and an understanding of how different herbs interact with the body and with each other. Here, we delve deeply into the nuanced world of selecting, blending, and brewing herbal teas, providing you with the knowledge to create potent, healing infusions.

Selecting and Blending Herbs

The foundation of crafting an herbal tea remedy lies in understanding the unique flavor profiles and medicinal properties of each herb. Herbs can range from sweet and floral, like chamomile and lavender, to earthy and bitter, like dandelion and burdock root. Recognizing these flavors is crucial not only for creating a pleasing cup of tea but also for harnessing the specific healing benefits you seek. Each herb carries its own set of health benefits, which can be combined synergistically in a blend. For instance, combining ginger, known for its warming and digestive properties, with peppermint, known for easing digestive discomfort, creates a blend that is both potent and palatable.

Tips for Creating Balanced and Effective Herbal Blends

1. **Start with a Purpose:** Define what you want your herbal tea to achieve. Are you looking to relieve stress, improve digestion, or boost your immune system? This will guide your selection of herbs.

2. **Research Herb Interactions:** Some herbs can interact with medications or affect specific health conditions negatively. Ensure the herbs you choose are safe for you.

3. **Balance Flavors:** Consider the flavor profiles of your chosen herbs. Aim for a balance between sweet, bitter, spicy, and sour to create a harmonious blend.

4. **Consider Proportions:** Start with a simple ratio of 1:1 when blending two herbs. Adjust according to taste and desired medicinal strength.

5. **Experiment:** Don't be afraid to experiment with different combinations. Small batches are perfect for testing and refining your blend.

Brewing Techniques

Crafting the perfect cup of herbal tea doesn't end with blending. The brewing process is equally important, as it's the stage where the herbs release their flavors and medicinal compounds into the water.

Guidelines for Extracting Maximum Benefits from Your Herbs

1. **Water Quality:** Begin with fresh, purified water to ensure no contaminants interfere with the tea's flavor and medicinal properties.

2. **Correct Temperature:** Different herbs require different brewing temperatures. Delicate herbs like chamomile flourish in just-boiled water, whereas roots and barks may need to be simmered to release their full potency.

3. **Cover While Steeping:** Covering your tea while it steeps prevents the escape of volatile oils and aromas, ensuring maximum flavor and therapeutic benefit.

4. **Steeping Time:** The time your herbs steep will affect the strength of the tea. Generally, 5-10 minutes is recommended, but tougher materials like roots may benefit from longer steeping.

The Importance of Temperature, Steeping Time, and Freshness

- **Temperature:** Too hot, and you risk destroying delicate compounds; too cool, and you may not extract the full spectrum of benefits. Learning the ideal temperature for each type of herb is key.

- **Steeping Time:** Over-steeping can lead to excessively bitter flavors, especially in tannin-rich herbs like green tea, while under-steeping might result in a weak infusion that lacks full medicinal value.

- **Freshness:** Using fresh, high-quality herbs is crucial. Dried herbs should be stored properly to preserve their potency. Look for vibrant colors and strong aromas as indicators of quality.

Crafting herbal tea remedies is a deeply rewarding practice that connects us to the natural world and to our own inner needs. It offers a moment of pause, an act of self-care, and a pathway to healing. With knowledge, care, and a spirit of exploration, you can unlock the vast potential of herbs and create personalized teas that nourish, heal, and delight.

Safety and Considerations in Herbal Tea Remedies

Embarking on the journey of crafting and consuming herbal tea remedies is not just about embracing the healing gifts of nature—it's also about understanding and respecting the potency and intricacies of herbs. As with any form of natural medicine, there are vital considerations to ensure that your herbal tea experience is both safe and beneficial.

Understanding Dosages and Interactions

Herbs, though natural, are not without their complexities. Each herb comes with its own set of active compounds, which can vary greatly in potency. The art of herbal tea making, therefore, requires a mindful approach to dosages and an awareness of potential interactions.

Dosage Awareness: Just as with conventional medicine, the principle of "dosage makes the poison" applies to herbs. Consuming herbal teas in moderation is key to harnessing their benefits while minimizing risks. For potent herbs, especially those with strong laxative or diuretic effects, sticking to recommended amounts is crucial to avoid adverse effects.

Herb-Drug Interactions: Some herbs can interact with prescription medications, either enhancing or inhibiting their effects. For example, St. John's Wort is known to interact with a wide range of medications, potentially diminishing their efficacy. Before incorporating a new herb into your routine, especially if you are on medication, it's essential to research potential interactions.

Condition-Specific Considerations: Certain herbs may not be suitable for individuals with specific health conditions. For instance, licorice root, while beneficial for many, can exacerbate hypertension and should be avoided by those with high blood pressure.

When to Consult with a Healthcare Provider

While herbal teas can be a valuable part of a wellness routine, they are not a substitute for professional medical advice. Consulting with a healthcare provider is particularly important in the following scenarios:

Existing Health Conditions: If you have a chronic health condition or are pregnant or breastfeeding, it's crucial to consult with a healthcare provider before adding herbal teas to your regimen.

Medication Interactions: If you're taking prescription or over-the-counter medications, a healthcare provider can advise on potential herb-drug interactions.

Severe or Persistent Symptoms: While herbal teas can provide relief for minor ailments, they are not equipped to treat serious or persistent health issues. Seek professional medical advice if symptoms worsen or do not improve.

Quality and Sourcing of Herbs

The efficacy and safety of your herbal tea remedies are directly influenced by the quality and sourcing of the herbs used. Understanding the distinction between organic and non-organic herbs, as well as knowing where and how the herbs are sourced, can significantly impact their healing potential.

Organic vs. Non-Organic: Organic herbs are grown without synthetic pesticides, herbicides, or fertilizers, minimizing your exposure to these chemicals. They often contain higher levels of beneficial compounds. Non-organic herbs, while sometimes more accessible and affordable, may carry residues of agricultural chemicals.

Quality Indicators: High-quality herbs are characterized by their vibrant color, potent aroma, and overall freshness. They should be sourced from reputable suppliers who prioritize sustainable and ethical harvesting practices. Look for certifications and third-party testing to ensure purity and potency.

Sustainability and Ethical Sourcing: Beyond personal health, the choice of herbs also impacts the health of the planet. Opting for herbs from sources that practice sustainable farming and ethical harvesting supports environmental stewardship and the well-being of communities involved in herb cultivation.

BOOST IMMUNE SYSTEM

1. Elderberry & Nettle Immune Booster Tea

Intended Use: This tea is a natural fortress, blending the mineral-rich nettle with antioxidant-packed elderberry to nurture your body's defense systems. A touch of honey and lemon not only delights the palate but also enhances the immune-boosting properties, making each cup a proactive step towards wellness.

Ingredients:

- 1 tbsp dried Elderberry

- 1 tbsp dried Stinging Nettle leaves

- 2 cups of boiling water

- 1 tsp raw Honey (optional, for sweetness)

- A slice of lemon (for vitamin C boost)

Instructions:

1. Place elderberries and nettle leaves in a tea infuser or teapot.

2. Pour boiling water over them and let steep for 15 minutes to extract all the vitamins and minerals.

3. Strain into a mug, then add honey and a slice of lemon to enhance flavor and vitamin C content.

4. Drink this tea daily to support overall immune health.

2. Ginger-Lemon Balm Immune Tea

Intended Use: Crafted for moments of need, this tea combines the invigorating warmth of ginger with the calming essence of lemon balm. Together, they create a soothing yet stimulating blend that supports the immune system and eases the mind, perfect for uplifting spirits and bolstering health.

Ingredients:

- 1 tsp fresh Ginger root, finely grated

- 1 tbsp Lemon balm leaves

- 2 cups of boiling water

- Honey to taste

Instructions:

1. Add ginger and lemon balm to a tea infuser or pot.

2. Pour boiling water over the herbs and steep for 10 minutes.

3. Strain and sweeten with honey as desired.

4. Enjoy this warming tea at the first sign of immune stress.

3. Echinacea & Dandelion Detox Tea

Intended Use: A purifying blend designed to support liver function and stimulate the immune system. Echinacea and dandelion join forces to detoxify and defend, offering a herbal solution for enhancing bodily resilience and promoting digestive health.

Ingredients:

- 1 tbsp dried Echinacea

- 1 tbsp dried Dandelion leaves

- 2 cups of water

- Lemon wedge for additional detoxification and flavor

Instructions:

1. Combine Echinacea and dandelion leaves in a pot with water and bring to a boil.

2. Reduce heat and simmer for about 15 minutes.

3. Strain the tea into a mug and add a squeeze of lemon.

4. Drink once daily to support the immune system and liver health.

4. Turmeric & Black Pepper Wellness Tea

Intended Use: This vibrant tea merges the anti-inflammatory prowess of turmeric with the absorption-enhancing effects of black pepper. Ideal for immune support and inflammation reduction, it's a therapeutic cup aimed at fostering overall health and vitality.

Ingredients:

- 1 tsp Turmeric powder

- A pinch of Black pepper (to enhance curcumin absorption)

- 1 tbsp Honey

- 2 cups of boiling water

- 1 tbsp Lemon juice

Instructions:

1. Dissolve turmeric and black pepper in boiling water.

2. Allow to steep for 10 minutes.

3. Strain into a cup, then stir in honey and lemon juice.

4. Consume this vibrant tea regularly to maintain a healthy immune response.

5. Astragalus & Peppermint Immune Tea

Intended Use: A blend that energizes and shields, combining astragalus's immune-boosting power with peppermint's refreshing vitality. This tea is designed to invigorate the senses while strengthening the body's natural defenses, making it a perfect companion for maintaining health and wellness.

Ingredients:

- 1 tbsp dried Astragalus root

- 1 tbsp dried Peppermint leaves

- 2 cups of boiling water

- Honey or lemon to taste

Instructions:

1. Place astragalus root and peppermint leaves in a tea infuser within a teapot.

2. Pour boiling water over the herbs and steep for about 20 minutes; astragalus needs longer to release its properties.

3. Strain, adding honey or lemon according to taste preference.

4. Drink this tea to enhance immune defense and energy levels.

STRESS RELIEF

6. Chamomile & Lavender Calm Tea

Intended Use: A serene blend designed to soothe the nervous system and ease the mind. Chamomile's gentle calming properties are perfectly complemented by lavender's stress-relieving essence, creating a peaceful haven in each cup. Ideal for unwinding after a long day or preparing for a restful night's sleep.

Ingredients:

- 1 tbsp dried Chamomile flowers
- 1 tsp dried Lavender buds
- 2 cups of boiling water
- Honey or lemon to taste

Instructions:

1. Place chamomile and lavender in a tea infuser or pot.
2. Pour boiling water over the herbs and let steep for 5-7 minutes.
3. Strain and add honey or lemon as desired.
4. Sip slowly and breathe deeply to invite tranquility and relaxation.

7. Lemon Balm & Mint Stress Relief Tea

Intended Use: A refreshing blend that targets stress and anxiety, promoting relaxation and mental clarity. Lemon balm, with its mood-enhancing properties, pairs wonderfully with mint to cool and calm the body and mind, making it an excellent choice for stress relief and improved focus.

Ingredients:

- 1 tbsp dried Lemon balm leaves
- 1 tbsp dried Mint leaves
- 2 cups of boiling water
- A slice of fresh lemon (optional)

Instructions:

1. Combine lemon balm and mint in a teapot.
2. Add boiling water and steep for 10 minutes.
3. Strain into a mug, adding a slice of lemon for a refreshing twist.
4. Enjoy anytime you need a mental lift or a moment of calm.

8. Passionflower & Valerian Soothe Tea

Intended Use: Crafted to deeply relax the mind and prepare the body for sleep, this blend harnesses the powerful sedative qualities of passionflower and valerian root. Perfect for those with restless minds, seeking a natural remedy for insomnia or stress-induced sleeplessness.

Ingredients:

- 1 tbsp dried Passionflower

- 1 tsp dried Valerian root

- 2 cups of boiling water

- Honey to sweeten (optional)

Instructions:

1. Mix passionflower and valerian root in a teapot.

2. Pour boiling water over the mixture and steep for 15 minutes.

3. Strain and sweeten with honey if needed.

4. Drink before bedtime as a peaceful sleep aid.

9. Ashwagandha & Ginger Relaxation Tea

Intended Use: A grounding blend aimed at reducing stress, anxiety, and inflammation. Ashwagandha provides strength and resilience to stress, while ginger adds a warming and digestive aid. This tea is ideal for those looking to restore balance and promote inner peace.

Ingredients:

- 1 tsp Ashwagandha powder

- 1 tsp fresh Ginger root, grated

- 2 cups of water

- 1 tsp Honey (optional)

Instructions:

1. Boil ginger and ashwagandha in water for 10 minutes.

2. Strain the tea into a mug and add honey to taste.

3. Drink in the evening to unwind or after meals to aid digestion and calm the mind.

10. Green Tea & Rosehip Serenity Tea

Intended Use: An antioxidant-rich blend that gently reduces stress while supporting overall health. Green tea provides a mild caffeine lift, enhanced by the vitamin C and anti-inflammatory properties of rosehips. This tea is perfect for a serene break in your day, offering a moment of calm and rejuvenation.

Ingredients:

- 1 tbsp Green tea leaves

- 1 tsp dried Rosehips

- 2 cups of boiling water

- Lemon wedge or honey to taste

Instructions:

1. Place green tea and rosehips in a teapot.

2. Pour boiling water over them and let steep for 3-5 minutes.

3. Strain and add a lemon wedge or honey as desired.

4. Enjoy this soothing blend whenever you need a stress-free moment or a gentle energy boost.

DIGESTIVE HEALTH

11. Dandelion & Peppermint Digestive Aid Tea

Intended Use: A soothing blend that stimulates digestion and supports liver health, leveraging the detoxifying properties of dandelion with the calming effects of peppermint.

Ingredients:

- 1 tbsp dried Dandelion leaves

- 1 tbsp dried Peppermint leaves

- 2 cups of boiling water

- Honey to taste

Instructions:

1. Combine dandelion and peppermint in a tea infuser or pot.

2. Pour boiling water over the herbs and let steep for 10 minutes.

3. Strain and sweeten with honey as desired.

4. Drink after meals to aid digestion and soothe the digestive tract.

12. Nettle & Ginger Mineral Rich Tea

Intended Use: This nutrient-dense tea combines the mineral richness of nettle with the digestive benefits of ginger, making it perfect for improving digestion and enhancing overall nutrient absorption.

Ingredients:

- 1 tbsp dried Stinging Nettle leaves

- 1 tsp fresh Ginger root, grated

- 2 cups of boiling water

- Lemon slice (optional for detox and flavor)

Instructions:

1. Place nettle and ginger in a teapot.

2. Add boiling water and steep for about 10 minutes.

3. Strain into a mug, adding a slice of lemon if desired.

4. Enjoy this tea daily to support digestive health and mineral intake.

13. Fennel & Lemon Balm Digestive Comfort Tea

Intended Use: A gentle, comforting tea aimed at easing digestive discomfort, reducing bloating, and promoting a healthy digestive system through the carminative properties of fennel and the soothing nature of lemon balm.

Ingredients:

- 1 tbsp dried Fennel seeds
- 1 tbsp dried Lemon balm leaves
- 2 cups of boiling water
- Honey or lemon to taste

Instructions:

1. Crush the fennel seeds lightly and mix with lemon balm leaves in a teapot.
2. Pour boiling water over and steep for 10 minutes.
3. Strain and add honey or lemon according to taste.
4. Sip slowly after meals to aid in digestion and relieve gastrointestinal distress.

14. Chamomile & Aloe Vera Soothing Tea

Intended Use: Designed to calm the digestive tract and promote healing of the gastrointestinal lining, this tea combines the soothing properties of chamomile with the regenerative benefits of aloe vera.

Ingredients:

- 1 tbsp dried Chamomile flowers
- 1 tbsp Aloe Vera juice
- 2 cups of hot water
- Honey to sweeten (optional)

Instructions:

1. Steep chamomile flowers in hot water for about 5-7 minutes.
2. Strain into a large mug and let it cool down a bit before adding aloe vera juice.
3. Sweeten with honey if desired.
4. Drink this tea to soothe the digestive system, especially after a heavy meal or when experiencing discomfort.

15. Licorice Root & Slippery Elm Bark Healing Tea

Intended Use: This tea is a powerhouse for digestive health, combining the soothing properties of slippery elm bark with the sweet, adrenal-supporting licorice root, ideal for healing and protecting the digestive tract.

Ingredients:

- 1 tsp dried Licorice root

- 1 tsp dried Slippery elm bark

- 2 cups of boiling water

- Cinnamon or honey to taste

Instructions:

1. Mix licorice root and slippery elm bark in a pot with water and bring to a simmer for about 15 minutes.

2. Strain the tea into a mug, adding cinnamon or honey to enhance flavor and benefits.

3. Drink this nurturing tea to support digestive health, particularly when feeling unwell or in need of digestive healing.

DETOXIFICATION/ CLEANSE BODY

16. Dandelion Root Detox Tea

Intended Use: Harnesses the liver-cleansing properties of dandelion root, making it an excellent choice for a natural detox. This tea aids in flushing toxins from the liver and kidneys, supporting overall body detoxification.

Ingredients:

- 2 tbsp dried Dandelion root
- 1 tbsp dried Burdock root
- 2 cups of boiling water
- Lemon slice for added detox benefits and flavor

Instructions:

1. Combine dandelion and burdock roots in a pot.
2. Add boiling water and simmer for 10 minutes to extract the full benefits.
3. Strain into a mug, adding a slice of lemon for a refreshing taste and vitamin C boost.
4. Drink in the morning or before bed to support the body's natural detox processes.

17. Green Tea & Nettle Cleansing Blend

Intended Use: A revitalizing tea that combines the antioxidant power of green tea with the mineral-rich and detoxifying properties of nettle, ideal for supporting the body's elimination processes and providing an energy boost.

Ingredients:

- 1 tbsp Green tea leaves
- 1 tbsp dried Stinging Nettle leaves
- 2 cups of hot water
- Honey or a dash of lemon to taste

Instructions:

1. Mix green tea and nettle leaves in a teapot.
2. Pour hot water over the herbs and let steep for 3-5 minutes.
3. Strain and add honey or lemon as desired for flavor.
4. Enjoy this tea in the morning to kickstart your day with a detoxifying boost.

18. Milk Thistle & Peppermint Liver Cleanse Tea

Intended Use: Combines the liver-supporting properties of milk thistle with the digestive aid of peppermint, creating a powerful detox tea that helps cleanse the liver and improve digestion.

Ingredients:

- 1 tbsp dried Milk Thistle seeds
- 1 tbsp dried Peppermint leaves
- 2 cups of boiling water
- Honey to sweeten (optional)

Instructions:

1. Crush milk thistle seeds slightly and mix with peppermint leaves in a tea infuser.
2. Pour boiling water over the herbs and steep for 15 minutes to ensure maximum extraction.
3. Strain into a mug and sweeten with honey if preferred.
4. Drink this tea daily to aid liver detoxification and support digestive health.

19. Cilantro & Lemon Detox Tea

Intended Use: Utilizes the heavy metal detoxifying properties of cilantro, paired with the cleansing power of lemon, to create a detox tea that helps rid the body of toxins and rejuvenates the system.

Ingredients:

- A handful of fresh Cilantro leaves
- 1 Lemon (juice)
- 2 cups of boiling water
- Honey (optional, for sweetness)

Instructions:

1. Place cilantro leaves in a pot and cover with boiling water.
2. Let steep for 10 minutes, then strain into a mug.
3. Squeeze in the juice of one lemon and add honey to taste if desired.
4. Drink this tea anytime you feel the need for a detoxifying boost or to aid in heavy metal cleansing.

20. Ginger & Turmeric Flush Tea

Intended Use: A potent tea that combines the digestive benefits of ginger with the anti-inflammatory and detoxifying effects of turmeric, perfect for cleansing the body and supporting digestive health.

Ingredients:

- 1 tsp fresh Ginger root, grated
- 1 tsp Turmeric powder or fresh Turmeric root, grated
- 2 cups of boiling water
- Black pepper (a pinch to enhance turmeric absorption)
- Honey or lemon to taste

Instructions:

1. Boil ginger and turmeric in water for 10 minutes to fully release their beneficial properties.

2. Strain the tea into a mug, adding a pinch of black pepper to enhance the bioavailability of curcumin in turmeric.

3. Sweeten with honey or lemon according to preference.

4. Sip this tea in the morning or evening to aid in the body's natural detoxification process and to combat inflammation.

IMPROVE SLEEP

21. Chamomile & Lavender Sleepy Time Tea

Intended Use: A classic blend that uses the soothing properties of chamomile and lavender to calm the nervous system and promote a peaceful night's sleep. Ideal for those evenings when you need help winding down.

Ingredients:

- 1 tbsp dried Chamomile flowers
- 1 tsp dried Lavender buds
- 2 cups of boiling water
- A spoonful of honey (optional, for sweetness)

Instructions:

1. Place chamomile and lavender in a tea infuser or pot.
2. Pour boiling water over the herbs and let steep for 5-7 minutes.
3. Strain and add honey as desired for a touch of sweetness.
4. Drink 30 minutes before bedtime to ease into a restful sleep.

22. Lemon Balm & Valerian Root Night Tea

Intended Use: Combines the stress-reducing effect of lemon balm with the powerful sedative qualities of valerian root, creating a potent tea to improve sleep quality and duration. Perfect for those with occasional insomnia.

Ingredients:

- 1 tbsp dried Lemon balm leaves
- 1 tsp dried Valerian root
- 2 cups of boiling water
- Lemon slice or honey to taste

Instructions:

1. Mix lemon balm and valerian root in a teapot.
2. Pour boiling water over the mixture and steep for 10 minutes.
3. Strain into a mug, adding a slice of lemon or honey for flavor.
4. Consume shortly before bed to help induce a deep and restorative sleep.

23. Passionflower & Hops Relaxation Tea

Intended Use: A tranquil blend that uses passionflower and hops for their calming effects on the mind and body, aiding in the reduction of sleep latency and nighttime awakenings. Suited for those seeking a natural remedy to enhance sleep quality.

Ingredients:

- 1 tbsp dried Passionflower
- 1 tsp dried Hops
- 2 cups of boiling water
- Honey (optional, to sweeten)

Instructions:

1. Combine passionflower and hops in a teapot or infuser.
2. Add boiling water and steep for 15 minutes to extract their full benefits.
3. Strain and sweeten with honey if preferred.
4. Enjoy this tea an hour before bedtime to prepare for a peaceful night.

24. Magnolia Bark & Ginger Soothe Tea

Intended Use: Leverages the sleep-promoting properties of magnolia bark, complemented by the digestive aid of ginger, to promote relaxation and ease into sleep, especially beneficial for those whose sleep issues stem from digestive discomfort.

Ingredients:

- 1 tsp dried Magnolia bark
- 1 tsp fresh Ginger root, grated
- 2 cups of water
- A dash of cinnamon or honey for flavor

Instructions:

1. Simmer magnolia bark and ginger in water for 15 minutes.
2. Strain the tea into a cup, adding cinnamon or honey to enhance the flavor profile.
3. Drink in the evening to settle the stomach and calm the mind before sleep.

25. Ashwagandha & Mint Stress Relief Tea

Intended Use: Utilizes ashwagandha for its adaptogenic qualities to reduce stress and balance the body, combined with the refreshing taste of mint to soothe and prepare the body for sleep. Ideal for those looking to reduce stress-related sleep disturbances.

Ingredients:

- 1 tsp Ashwagandha powder

- 1 tbsp dried Mint leaves

- 2 cups of boiling water

- Honey or lemon to taste

Instructions:

1. Boil ashwagandha and mint leaves together for about 10 minutes.

2. Strain the mixture into a mug, adding honey or lemon as desired.

3. Enjoy this tea after dinner or before bed to support a calm state of mind and a restful night.

INCREASE ENERGY

26. Green Tea & Ginseng Vitality Boost

Intended Use: Combines the antioxidant-rich green tea with the energizing effects of ginseng, creating a stimulating blend that boosts mental and physical energy levels. Ideal for mornings or mid-afternoon slumps.

Ingredients:

- 1 tbsp Green tea leaves
- 1 tsp Ginseng root, finely sliced
- 2 cups of boiling water
- Honey or lemon to taste

Instructions:

1. Place green tea leaves and ginseng root in a teapot or infuser.
2. Pour boiling water over the mixture and let steep for 3-5 minutes.
3. Strain into a cup, adding honey or lemon according to preference.
4. Drink in the morning or early afternoon for an energy boost without the jitters.

27. Peppermint & Rosemary Focus Tea

Intended Use: A refreshing blend that sharpens focus and invigorates the senses, using peppermint for its stimulating properties and rosemary for its cognitive benefits. Perfect for enhancing concentration and energy.

Ingredients:

- 1 tbsp dried Peppermint leaves
- 1 tsp dried Rosemary
- 2 cups of boiling water
- A slice of fresh lemon (optional)

Instructions:

1. Combine peppermint and rosemary in a teapot.
2. Add boiling water and steep for 7-10 minutes.
3. Strain and add a slice of lemon for an extra zest.
4. Enjoy this tea during work or study sessions for improved focus and energy.

28. Yerba Mate & Lemon Energizer Tea

Intended Use: Utilizes the naturally caffeinated yerba mate to provide a sustained energy lift, complemented by lemon for its refreshing flavor and vitamin C boost. A great alternative to coffee for those seeking a balanced and healthy energy source.

Ingredients:

- 2 tbsp Yerba Mate leaves

- 2 cups of hot water

- Juice of ½ a lemon

- Honey to sweeten (optional)

Instructions:

1. Steep yerba mate in hot water for 5 minutes.

2. Strain into a mug and add fresh lemon juice.

3. Sweeten with honey if desired.

4. Drink in the morning or before physical activity for an energy boost.

29. Ashwagandha & Licorice Root Adaptogen Tea

Intended Use: A balancing blend that combines the adaptogenic power of ashwagandha with the sweet, sustaining energy of licorice root. This tea is designed to support stamina and energy levels while reducing stress.

Ingredients:

- 1 tsp Ashwagandha powder

- 1 tsp dried Licorice root

- 2 cups of boiling water

- Cinnamon or cardamom for flavor (optional)

Instructions:

1. Simmer ashwagandha and licorice root in water for 10-15 minutes.

2. Strain into a cup and add cinnamon or cardamom to taste.

3. Drink in the morning to energize your day or when you need a stress-free energy lift.

30. Hibiscus & Beetroot Power Tea

Intended Use: A vibrant and nutrient-rich tea that combines the natural stamina-enhancing properties of beetroot with the antioxidant benefits of hibiscus. This tea is perfect for a pre-workout energy boost or whenever you need a refreshing lift.

Ingredients:

- 1 tbsp dried Hibiscus flowers
- 1 tsp Beetroot powder
- 2 cups of hot water
- Honey or lemon to taste

Instructions:

1. Mix hibiscus flowers and beetroot powder in a teapot.
2. Pour hot water over the mixture and let steep for 5 minutes.
3. Strain into a cup, adding honey or lemon as preferred.
4. Enjoy this brightly colored, energizing tea to support physical performance and vitality.

WEIGHT LOSS SUPPORT

31. Green Tea & Cinnamon Metabolism Booster

Intended Use: Leverages the metabolism-boosting properties of green tea combined with the blood sugar-stabilizing effects of cinnamon. This tea is perfect for enhancing metabolic rate and supporting weight loss efforts.

Ingredients:

- 1 tbsp Green tea leaves

- 1 tsp Cinnamon bark or ½ tsp ground cinnamon

- 2 cups of boiling water

- A slice of fresh lemon (optional, for detoxification and flavor)

Instructions:

1. Place green tea leaves and cinnamon in a teapot or infuser.

2. Pour boiling water over them and let steep for 3-5 minutes.

3. Strain into a cup and add a slice of lemon if desired.

4. Drink in the morning to kickstart your metabolism or before meals to aid digestion and control appetite.

32. Dandelion & Lemon Detox Tea

Intended Use: Utilizes the natural diuretic properties of dandelion combined with the cleansing benefits of lemon. This tea supports detoxification and may help in reducing water retention, contributing to weight loss goals.

Ingredients:

- 1 tbsp dried Dandelion leaves

- Juice of 1 lemon

- 2 cups of boiling water

- Honey to taste (optional)

Instructions:

1. Steep dandelion leaves in boiling water for 10 minutes.

2. Strain the tea into a cup and add fresh lemon juice.

3. Sweeten with honey if desired.

4. Enjoy this tea throughout the day to support detoxification and hydration.

33. Fennel & Peppermint Appetite Suppressant Tea

Intended Use: A soothing blend that combines the appetite-suppressing properties of fennel with the digestive benefits of peppermint. This tea is ideal for reducing cravings and supporting digestive health, aiding in weight loss.

Ingredients:

- 1 tbsp dried Fennel seeds

- 1 tbsp dried Peppermint leaves

- 2 cups of boiling water

- A pinch of ground ginger (optional, for additional metabolic support)

Instructions:

1. Crush fennel seeds lightly and mix with peppermint leaves in a teapot.

2. Add boiling water and steep for 7-10 minutes.

3. Strain and add a pinch of ground ginger if using.

4. Drink before meals to help reduce appetite and enhance digestion.

34. Hibiscus & Berries Fat-Burning Tea

Intended Use: Features the antioxidant-rich hibiscus and a blend of berries to stimulate fat burning and offer a delicious, low-calorie drink. This tea is perfect for satisfying sweet cravings while supporting weight loss.

Ingredients:

- 1 tbsp dried Hibiscus flowers

- 1 tbsp mixed dried berries (raspberries, blueberries, strawberries)

- 2 cups of hot water

- Honey to taste (optional)

Instructions:

1. Combine hibiscus flowers and mixed berries in a teapot.

2. Pour hot water over the mixture and let steep for 5 minutes.

3. Strain into a cup and sweeten with honey as desired.

4. Enjoy this fruity tea as a refreshing, fat-burning treat during the day.

35. Ginger & Turmeric Slimming Tea

Intended Use: A potent blend that harnesses the digestive-enhancing and anti-inflammatory properties of ginger and turmeric. This tea aids in boosting metabolism and reducing bloat, supporting weight loss efforts.

Ingredients:

- 1 tsp fresh Ginger root, grated

- 1 tsp Turmeric powder or fresh Turmeric root, grated

- 2 cups of boiling water

- Black pepper (a pinch to enhance turmeric absorption)

- Lemon juice or honey to taste

Instructions:

1. Boil ginger and turmeric in water for 10 minutes.

2. Strain the tea into a cup, adding a pinch of black pepper to enhance absorption.

3. Add lemon juice or honey according to taste preference.

4. Drink in the morning on an empty stomach or before meals to stimulate digestion and support weight management.

SKIN HEALTH

36. Nettle & Chamomile Skin Soothe Tea

Intended Use: Combines the mineral-rich stinging nettle with the calming properties of chamomile to nourish and soothe the skin from within. This tea is perfect for reducing inflammation and promoting a healthy, glowing complexion.

Ingredients:

- 1 tbsp dried Stinging Nettle leaves

- 1 tbsp dried Chamomile flowers

- 2 cups of boiling water

- Honey to taste (optional)

Instructions:

1. Mix nettle and chamomile in a teapot or infuser.

2. Pour boiling water over the herbs and let steep for 10 minutes.

3. Strain into a cup and add honey if desired for sweetness.

4. Drink daily to support skin health and reduce skin irritation.

37. Dandelion & Burdock Clear Skin Tea

Intended Use: Leverages the detoxifying properties of dandelion and burdock root to cleanse the blood and liver, promoting clear skin and aiding in the reduction of acne and skin blemishes.

Ingredients:

- 1 tbsp dried Dandelion root

- 1 tbsp dried Burdock root

- 2.5 cups of water

- Lemon wedge for flavor and vitamin C

Instructions:

1. Combine dandelion and burdock roots in a pot with water.

2. Bring to a boil, then simmer for 15 minutes.

3. Strain the tea into a mug, squeezing in the lemon wedge.

4. Consume this tea twice daily to help clear skin from the inside out.

38. Green Tea & Mint Antioxidant Tea

Intended Use: A refreshing tea rich in antioxidants from green tea, enhanced with the cooling properties of mint. This blend is designed to protect the skin against oxidative stress and improve skin vitality.

Ingredients:

- 1 tbsp Green tea leaves
- 1 tbsp dried Mint leaves
- 2 cups of hot water
- A slice of cucumber for added hydration and skin benefits

Instructions:

1. Steep green tea and mint leaves in hot water for 3-5 minutes.
2. Strain into a cup and add a slice of cucumber for a refreshing touch.
3. Drink daily to enjoy the antioxidant benefits and support healthy, vibrant skin.

39. Aloe Vera & Lemon Balm Healing Tea

Intended Use: Combines the gastrointestinal soothing effects of aloe vera with the calming properties of lemon balm to promote skin healing and reduce inflammation from within, supporting overall skin health.

Ingredients:

- 1 tbsp Aloe Vera juice
- 1 tbsp dried Lemon balm leaves
- 2 cups of boiling water
- Honey or lemon to taste

Instructions:

1. Steep lemon balm leaves in boiling water for 10 minutes.
2. Strain the tea into a mug and let it cool slightly before adding aloe vera juice.
3. Sweeten with honey or lemon as desired.
4. Drink regularly to aid in skin repair and to maintain a healthy, soothing effect on the skin.

40. Cucumber & Parsley Detox Tea

Intended Use: A hydrating and detoxifying blend that uses cucumber and parsley, known for their skin-cleansing properties. This tea helps to flush toxins from the body, contributing to clearer and more hydrated skin.

Ingredients:

- ½ fresh Cucumber, sliced

- A handful of fresh Parsley

- 2 cups of boiling water

- A dash of lemon juice for extra detoxification and taste

Instructions:

1. Place cucumber slices and parsley in a large mug or pitcher.

2. Pour boiling water over the **Ingredients** and let steep for 10-15 minutes.

3. Strain into a cup, adding a dash of lemon juice.

4. Enjoy this tea cold or at room temperature throughout the day for maximum hydration and skin benefits.

HEART HEALTH

41. Hawthorn & Rosehip Heart Tonic Tea

Intended Use: Utilizes the cardiovascular benefits of hawthorn berries, known for their ability to strengthen and protect heart function, combined with vitamin C-rich rosehips to support blood vessel health and circulation.

Ingredients:

- 1 tbsp dried Hawthorn berries
- 1 tbsp dried Rosehips
- 2 cups of boiling water
- Honey to taste (optional)

Instructions:

1. Mix hawthorn berries and rosehips in a teapot or infuser.
2. Pour boiling water over the herbs and let steep for 15 minutes to extract their full benefits.
3. Strain into a cup and add honey if desired for sweetness.
4. Drink daily to support heart health and circulation.

42. Green Tea & Ginger Cardiovascular Blend

Intended Use: A powerful blend that combines the antioxidant properties of green tea with the circulation-boosting effects of ginger, promoting arterial health and reducing the risk of cardiovascular diseases.

Ingredients:

- 1 tbsp Green tea leaves
- 1 tsp fresh Ginger root, grated
- 2 cups of hot water
- A slice of lemon (optional, for detoxification and flavor)

Instructions:

1. Steep green tea and ginger in hot water for 3-5 minutes.
2. Strain into a cup, adding a slice of lemon if desired.
3. Enjoy this tea in the morning or early afternoon to boost heart health and provide antioxidant protection.

43. Dandelion & Lemon Balm Heart Health Tea

Intended Use: Combines the diuretic properties of dandelion with the calming effects of lemon balm, aiding in blood pressure management and providing a soothing effect on the heart.

Ingredients:

- 1 tbsp dried Dandelion leaves
- 1 tbsp dried Lemon balm leaves
- 2 cups of boiling water
- Honey or lemon to taste

Instructions:

1. Place dandelion and lemon balm in a tea infuser or pot.
2. Pour boiling water over the herbs and let steep for 10 minutes.
3. Strain and add honey or lemon according to preference.
4. Drink regularly to support heart function and blood pressure regulation.

44. Bilberry & Hibiscus Antioxidant Tea

Intended Use: A delicious blend rich in antioxidants from bilberries and hibiscus, known for their role in improving heart health by reducing oxidative stress and supporting healthy blood pressure levels.

Ingredients:

- 1 tbsp dried Bilberries
- 1 tbsp dried Hibiscus flowers
- 2 cups of boiling water
- Honey to sweeten (optional)

Instructions:

1. Combine bilberries and hibiscus in a teapot.
2. Pour boiling water over the mixture and steep for 5-7 minutes.
3. Strain into a cup and sweeten with honey as desired.
4. Drink this tea daily to enjoy its heart-protective benefits.

45. Turmeric & Cinnamon Circulation Support Tea

Intended Use: Utilizes the anti-inflammatory and blood-thinning properties of turmeric, combined with the blood sugar-stabilizing effects of cinnamon, to support heart health and improve circulation.

Ingredients:

- 1 tsp Turmeric powder (or 1 tbsp grated fresh turmeric root)
- 1 tsp Cinnamon bark or ½ tsp ground cinnamon
- 2 cups of boiling water
- Black pepper (a pinch to enhance turmeric absorption)
- Honey or lemon to taste

Instructions:

1. Boil turmeric and cinnamon in water for 10 minutes.
2. Strain the tea into a cup, adding a pinch of black pepper to enhance absorption.
3. Add honey or lemon according to taste preference.
4. Consume this warming tea regularly to support heart health and circulation.

ANTI INFLAMMATORY

46. Turmeric & Ginger Inflammation Soother Tea

Intended Use: Combines the potent anti-inflammatory effects of turmeric with the warming relief of ginger, creating a powerful tea to soothe inflammation and reduce discomfort.

Ingredients:

- 1 tsp Turmeric powder (or 1 tbsp grated fresh turmeric root)
- 1 tsp fresh Ginger root, grated
- 2 cups of boiling water
- A pinch of black pepper (to enhance curcumin absorption)
- Honey or lemon to taste

Instructions:

1. Boil turmeric and ginger in water for 10 minutes.
2. Strain the tea into a cup, adding a pinch of black pepper to enhance the bioavailability of curcumin from turmeric.
3. Sweeten with honey or add lemon according to taste preference.
4. Drink this tea 1-2 times daily to combat inflammation throughout the body.

47. Chamomile & Lavender Anti-Stress Tea

Intended Use: Utilizes the calming properties of chamomile and lavender to reduce stress-induced inflammation, promoting relaxation and a sense of well-being.

Ingredients:

- 1 tbsp dried Chamomile flowers
- 1 tsp dried Lavender buds
- 2 cups of boiling water
- Honey to taste (optional)

Instructions:

1. Place chamomile and lavender in a tea infuser or pot.
2. Pour boiling water over the herbs and let steep for 5-7 minutes.
3. Strain and add honey as desired for sweetness.
4. Enjoy in the evening or whenever stress levels are high to aid relaxation and reduce inflammation.

48. Pineapple & Mint Digestive Aid Tea

Intended Use: A refreshing tea featuring bromelain-rich pineapple for its digestive and anti-inflammatory benefits, paired with mint to soothe the digestive tract.

Ingredients:

- ½ cup fresh Pineapple, chopped
- 1 tbsp dried Mint leaves
- 2 cups of boiling water
- A splash of lemon juice (optional, for extra flavor and vitamin C)

Instructions:

1. Add pineapple and mint leaves to a teapot or large mug.
2. Pour boiling water over the **Ingredients** and let steep for 10 minutes.
3. Strain into a cup, adding a splash of lemon juice if using.
4. Drink after meals to support digestion and combat inflammation.

49. Rosehip & Hibiscus Vitamin C Boost Tea

Intended Use: Leverages the high vitamin C content of rosehip and the antioxidant properties of hibiscus to support immune health and reduce inflammation.

Ingredients:

- 1 tbsp dried Rosehips
- 1 tbsp dried Hibiscus flowers
- 2 cups of boiling water
- Honey to sweeten (optional)

Instructions:

1. Mix rosehips and hibiscus flowers in a teapot.
2. Pour boiling water over and steep for 5-7 minutes.
3. Strain into a cup and sweeten with honey as desired.
4. Drink this tea daily to enjoy its anti-inflammatory benefits and boost your vitamin C intake.

50. Green Tea & Cinnamon Antioxidant Tea

Intended Use: A synergistic blend that combines the antioxidant power of green tea with the anti-inflammatory benefits of cinnamon, aiding in reducing inflammation and supporting overall health.

Ingredients:

- 1 tbsp Green tea leaves

- 1 tsp Cinnamon bark or ½ tsp ground cinnamon

- 2 cups of boiling water

- A slice of fresh ginger (optional, for added anti-inflammatory effect)

Instructions:

1. Place green tea leaves and cinnamon in a teapot or infuser.

2. Add a slice of fresh ginger if desired.

3. Pour boiling water over the mixture and let steep for 3-5 minutes.

4. Strain into a cup and enjoy warm.

5. Consume this tea in the morning or throughout the day to harness its antioxidant and anti-inflammatory properties.

BLOOD SUGAR REGULATION

51. Cinnamon & Fenugreek Balance Tea

Intended Use: Leverages the blood sugar-lowering properties of cinnamon and fenugreek, creating a potent blend that helps to regulate glucose levels and improve insulin sensitivity.

Ingredients:

- 1 tsp ground Cinnamon
- 1 tsp Fenugreek seeds, slightly crushed
- 2 cups of boiling water
- Honey or lemon to taste (optional)

Instructions:

1. Combine cinnamon and fenugreek seeds in a teapot or infuser.
2. Pour boiling water over the herbs and let steep for 10 minutes.
3. Strain into a cup and add honey or lemon as desired for flavor.
4. Drink this tea in the morning to help stabilize blood sugar levels throughout the day.

52. Green Tea & Bitter Melon Metabolic Support Tea

Intended Use: Combines the metabolic-boosting effects of green tea with the glucose-regulating benefits of bitter melon, offering support for those looking to manage their blood sugar levels naturally.

Ingredients:

- 1 tbsp Green tea leaves
- 1 tbsp Bitter melon, chopped (fresh or dried)
- 2.5 cups of water
- A slice of lemon (optional, for added flavor and vitamin C)

Instructions:

1. Add green tea leaves and bitter melon to a pot of water and bring to a simmer.
2. Let the mixture simmer for 5 minutes, then steep for an additional 5 minutes off the heat.
3. Strain the tea into a mug, adding a slice of lemon if desired.
4. Enjoy once daily, preferably in the morning, to aid blood sugar regulation.

53. Dandelion & Peppermint Liver Detox Tea

Intended Use: Utilizes the detoxifying properties of dandelion root and the soothing effects of peppermint to support liver health, an important aspect of maintaining balanced blood sugar levels.

Ingredients:

- 1 tbsp dried Dandelion root
- 1 tbsp dried Peppermint leaves
- 2 cups of boiling water
- Honey to sweeten (optional)

Instructions:

1. Mix dandelion root and peppermint leaves in a teapot or infuser.
2. Pour boiling water over the mixture and let steep for 10-15 minutes.
3. Strain and sweeten with honey if desired.
4. Drink daily, especially after meals, to support digestion and liver function, both crucial for blood sugar management.

54. Ginger & Turmeric Anti-Inflammatory Tea

Intended Use: Features ginger and turmeric for their anti-inflammatory and blood sugar-lowering effects, helping to reduce insulin resistance and support metabolic health.

Ingredients:

- 1 tsp fresh Ginger root, grated
- 1 tsp Turmeric powder (or 1 tbsp grated fresh turmeric root)
- 2 cups of boiling water
- A pinch of black pepper (to enhance turmeric absorption)
- Lemon or honey to taste

Instructions:

1. Boil ginger and turmeric in water for 10 minutes.
2. Strain the tea into a cup, adding a pinch of black pepper to enhance absorption.
3. Add lemon or honey according to taste preference.
4. Consume this warming tea regularly to help manage inflammation and blood sugar levels.

55. Licorice Root & Cinnamon Sweet Cravings Tea

Intended Use: A sweet, satisfying tea that uses the natural sweetness of licorice root to curb sugar cravings, along with cinnamon for its blood sugar regulation properties, making it an ideal choice for those monitoring their glucose levels.

Ingredients:

- 1 tsp Licorice root

- 1 tsp ground Cinnamon

- 2 cups of boiling water

- A drop of vanilla extract (optional, for enhanced flavor)

Instructions:

1. Combine licorice root and cinnamon in a teapot or infuser.

2. Pour boiling water over the herbs and let steep for 10 minutes.

3. Strain into a cup and add a drop of vanilla extract if using.

4. Drink this tea when cravings strike to support blood sugar regulation and satisfy sweet tooth naturally.

RESPIRATORY HEALTH

56. Thyme & Licorice Root Respiratory Relief Tea

Intended Use: Combines the expectorant properties of thyme with the soothing effects of licorice root, creating a potent blend that helps ease coughing and supports healthy respiratory function.

Ingredients:

- 1 tbsp dried Thyme leaves

- 1 tsp Licorice root, chopped

- 2 cups of boiling water

- Honey to taste (optional, for additional soothing effect)

Instructions:

1. Place thyme and licorice root in a teapot or infuser.

2. Pour boiling water over the herbs and let steep for 10-15 minutes.

3. Strain into a cup and sweeten with honey if desired.

4. Drink up to 2 times daily, especially during cold weather or when experiencing respiratory discomfort.

57. Eucalyptus & Peppermint Clear Airways Tea

Intended Use: Utilizes the decongestant properties of eucalyptus and peppermint to clear airways, relieve congestion, and promote easier breathing.

Ingredients:

- 1 tbsp dried Eucalyptus leaves

- 1 tbsp dried Peppermint leaves

- 2 cups of boiling water

- A slice of lemon (optional, for added vitamin C and flavor)

Instructions:

1. Mix eucalyptus and peppermint leaves in a teapot or infuser.

2. Pour boiling water over and let steep for 10 minutes.

3. Strain into a mug, adding a slice of lemon if desired.

4. Inhale the steam before drinking to help clear the nasal passages, then drink to soothe the throat and chest.

58. Mullein & Marshmallow Leaf Soothing Tea

Intended Use: A gentle tea that blends the softening and soothing properties of marshmallow leaf with the respiratory support offered by mullein, ideal for calming irritated airways and supporting overall lung health.

Ingredients:

- 1 tbsp dried Mullein leaves
- 1 tbsp dried Marshmallow leaves
- 2.5 cups of water
- Honey or lemon to taste

Instructions:

1. Place mullein and marshmallow leaves in a pot with water and bring to a simmer.
2. Reduce heat and simmer for 15 minutes to fully extract the mucilaginous and beneficial compounds.
3. Strain the tea into a cup, adding honey or lemon according to taste.
4. Drink 1-2 times daily to support respiratory health, especially when feeling under the weather.

59. Ginger & Honey Bronchial Support Tea

Intended Use: Offers bronchial support with the warming and anti-inflammatory properties of ginger, enhanced by the natural antibacterial and soothing effects of honey, to support respiratory health and ease breathing.

Ingredients:

- 1 tsp fresh Ginger root, grated
- 2 cups of boiling water
- 1 tbsp Honey (preferably raw and organic)
- A dash of lemon juice (optional, for extra immune support)

Instructions:

1. Steep grated ginger in boiling water for 10 minutes.
2. Strain the tea into a mug and stir in honey and a dash of lemon juice if using.
3. Drink warm to help soothe the throat, reduce inflammation, and support healthy airways.

60. Elderberry & Rosehip Immune Boosting Tea

Intended Use: A vitamin C-rich tea that combines the immune-boosting benefits of elderberry and rosehip, supporting respiratory health and helping the body resist and recover from colds and flu.

Ingredients:

- 1 tbsp dried Elderberries

- 1 tbsp dried Rosehips

- 2.5 cups of water

- Honey to sweeten (optional)

Instructions:

1. Add elderberries and rosehips to a pot of water and bring to a boil.

2. Reduce heat and simmer for about 15 minutes to extract all the beneficial properties.

3. Strain the tea into a mug, sweetening as desired.

4. Enjoy this immune-boosting tea during cold and flu season or whenever additional respiratory support is needed.

JOINT AND MUSCLE RELIEF

61. Turmeric & Ginger Anti-Inflammatory Tea

Intended Use: Combines the powerful anti-inflammatory benefits of turmeric and ginger, offering relief from joint pain and muscle soreness. This tea is ideal for reducing inflammation and promoting recovery.

Ingredients:

- 1 tsp Turmeric powder (or 1 tbsp grated fresh turmeric root)
- 1 tsp fresh Ginger root, grated
- 2 cups of boiling water
- A pinch of black pepper (to enhance curcumin absorption)
- Honey or lemon to taste

Instructions:

1. Boil turmeric and ginger in water for 10 minutes.
2. Strain the tea into a cup, adding a pinch of black pepper to enhance the absorption of turmeric's active compound, curcumin.
3. Add honey or lemon according to taste preference.
4. Drink this tea daily to support joint health and reduce inflammation.

62. Willow Bark & Chamomile Pain Relief Tea

Intended Use: Utilizes willow bark, known as nature's aspirin, in combination with the soothing properties of chamomile to relieve pain and discomfort associated with joint and muscle issues.

Ingredients:

- 1 tsp Willow bark
- 1 tbsp dried Chamomile flowers
- 2 cups of boiling water
- Honey to taste (optional)

Instructions:

1. Combine willow bark and chamomile in a teapot or infuser.
2. Pour boiling water over the mixture and let steep for 15 minutes.
3. Strain into a cup and add honey if desired for sweetness.

4. Consume once or twice daily to help alleviate pain and inflammation.

63. Nettle & Peppermint Refreshing Relief Tea

Intended Use: Features stinging nettle for its anti-inflammatory properties and peppermint for its cooling and soothing effect, making it a refreshing choice for those with joint and muscle discomfort.

Ingredients:

- 1 tbsp dried Stinging Nettle leaves
- 1 tbsp dried Peppermint leaves
- 2 cups of boiling water
- Lemon slice (optional, for flavor and vitamin C)

Instructions:

1. Mix nettle and peppermint leaves in a teapot or infuser.
2. Pour boiling water over and let steep for 10 minutes.
3. Strain into a mug, adding a slice of lemon if desired.
4. Drink regularly to enjoy the anti-inflammatory and soothing benefits for joints and muscles.

64. Rosemary & Lavender Muscle Soothe Tea

Intended Use: Aromatic rosemary and lavender are paired to create a tea that not only helps to reduce inflammation but also soothes the mind and body, aiding in the relaxation of tense muscles.

Ingredients:

- 1 tbsp dried Rosemary
- 1 tsp dried Lavender buds
- 2 cups of boiling water
- Honey to sweeten (optional)

Instructions:

1. Combine rosemary and lavender in a teapot or infuser.
2. Pour boiling water over the herbs and let steep for about 5-7 minutes.
3. Strain into a cup and sweeten as desired.
4. Sip in the evening or after physical activity to relax both body and mind.

65. Arnica & Eucalyptus Soothing Tea

Intended Use: Arnica is renowned for its ability to reduce bruising and swelling, while eucalyptus provides a cooling effect, together offering a soothing tea for external use on sore joints and muscles.

Ingredients:

- 1 tsp dried Arnica flowers (Note: Arnica is for external use only)
- 1 tbsp dried Eucalyptus leaves
- 2 cups of boiling water

Instructions:

1. Steep arnica flowers and eucalyptus leaves in boiling water for 15 minutes.

2. Allow the tea to cool to a safe temperature.

3. Apply the tea with a clean cloth as a compress to affected areas to help soothe sore muscles and joints. Do not consume this tea; it is for external use only.

MENTAL CLARITY AND FOCUS

66. Rosemary & Lemon Balm Clarity Tea

Intended Use: Combines the cognitive-enhancing properties of rosemary with the calming effects of lemon balm, creating a blend that sharpens focus while reducing stress, ideal for studying or intensive work periods.

Ingredients:

- 1 tbsp dried Rosemary leaves
- 1 tbsp dried Lemon balm leaves
- 2 cups of boiling water
- Honey or lemon to taste

Instructions:

1. Place rosemary and lemon balm in a teapot or infuser.
2. Pour boiling water over the herbs and let steep for 10 minutes.
3. Strain into a cup, adding honey or lemon according to preference.
4. Drink in the morning or before tasks that require enhanced focus and mental clarity.

67. Ginkgo Biloba & Green Tea Brain Boost Tea

Intended Use: Utilizes ginkgo biloba, known for improving blood circulation to the brain, in combination with the mild caffeine and antioxidant properties of green tea, to enhance cognitive function and alertness.

Ingredients:

- 1 tbsp dried Ginkgo biloba leaves
- 1 tbsp Green tea leaves
- 2 cups of hot water
- A slice of fresh ginger (optional, for added stimulation and flavor)

Instructions:

1. Mix ginkgo biloba and green tea leaves in a teapot or infuser.
2. Add a slice of fresh ginger if desired.
3. Pour hot water over the mixture and let steep for 3-5 minutes.

4. Strain into a cup and enjoy when you need a mental lift or before engaging in activities that require sharp focus.

68. Peppermint & Gotu Kola Energizing Focus Tea

Intended Use: A refreshing and stimulating blend that combines the mental clarity benefits of gotu kola with the invigorating properties of peppermint, providing a natural energy boost and enhancing concentration.

Ingredients:

- 1 tbsp dried Peppermint leaves
- 1 tsp dried Gotu kola leaves
- 2 cups of boiling water
- Honey to sweeten (optional)

Instructions:

1. Combine peppermint and gotu kola in a teapot or infuser.
2. Pour boiling water over the herbs and let steep for 10 minutes.
3. Strain into a cup and sweeten with honey if desired.
4. Drink during the afternoon slump or whenever you need to refresh your mind and restore focus.

69. Sage & Thyme Memory Tea

Intended Use: Features sage, known for its memory-enhancing effects, and thyme, which contains compounds beneficial for cognitive function, creating a tea that supports memory recall and brain health.

Ingredients:

- 1 tbsp dried Sage leaves
- 1 tsp dried Thyme leaves
- 2 cups of boiling water
- Lemon slice (optional, for taste and additional cognitive benefits)

Instructions:

1. Place sage and thyme in a tea infuser or pot.
2. Pour boiling water over the herbs and steep for about 5-7 minutes.
3. Strain and add a slice of lemon if desired.

4. Consume in the morning or before learning activities to enhance memory and cognitive performance.

70. Ashwagandha & Chamomile Calm Focus Tea

Intended Use: Blends the adaptogenic properties of ashwagandha, which helps reduce stress and anxiety, with the soothing effects of chamomile, promoting a calm yet focused state ideal for deep concentration tasks.

Ingredients:

- 1 tsp Ashwagandha powder
- 1 tbsp dried Chamomile flowers
- 2 cups of water
- Honey to sweeten (optional)

Instructions:

1. Simmer ashwagandha powder in water for 10 minutes.
2. Remove from heat, add chamomile flowers, and cover to steep for another 5 minutes.
3. Strain into a mug, sweetening as desired.
4. Drink in the evening or during periods of high stress to support a calm, focused mindset.

MOOD ENHANCEMENT

71. St. John's Wort & Lemon Balm Bliss Tea

Intended Use: Combines the mood-lifting properties of St. John's Wort with the calming effects of lemon balm, creating a soothing blend that helps alleviate mild depression and anxiety, promoting a sense of well-being.

Ingredients:

- 1 tsp dried St. John's Wort
- 1 tbsp dried Lemon balm leaves
- 2 cups of boiling water
- Honey to taste (optional)

Instructions:

1. Mix St. John's Wort and lemon balm in a teapot or infuser.
2. Pour boiling water over the herbs and let steep for 10 minutes.
3. Strain into a cup and sweeten with honey if desired.
4. Enjoy this tea in the afternoon or whenever you need a mood boost.

Note: Consult a healthcare provider before using St. John's Wort, as it can interact with certain medications.

72. Chamomile & Lavender Calm Tea

Intended Use: A gentle, soothing tea that uses the calming properties of chamomile and lavender to ease stress and anxiety, perfect for unwinding after a long day and promoting a positive mood.

Ingredients:

- 1 tbsp dried Chamomile flowers
- 1 tsp dried Lavender buds
- 2 cups of boiling water
- A slice of lemon (optional, for added flavor and vitamin C)

Instructions:

1. Place chamomile and lavender in a tea infuser or pot.
2. Pour boiling water over the herbs and let steep for 5-7 minutes.
3. Strain and add a slice of lemon if desired.

4. Drink in the evening to relax and uplift your mood before bedtime.

73. Peppermint & Rosehip Cheerful Tea

Intended Use: A vibrant, refreshing blend that combines the digestive and invigorating benefits of peppermint with the vitamin C-rich rosehips, energizing the body and elevating the mood.

Ingredients:

- 1 tbsp dried Peppermint leaves

- 1 tbsp dried Rosehips

- 2 cups of boiling water

- Honey to sweeten (optional)

Instructions:

1. Combine peppermint and rosehips in a teapot or infuser.

2. Pour boiling water over and let steep for 10 minutes.

3. Strain into a cup and sweeten as desired.

4. Enjoy this tea anytime for a refreshing mood boost and a burst of energy.

74. Ginseng & Green Tea Vitality Blend

Intended Use: Features ginseng for its energy-boosting and mood-enhancing effects, paired with the antioxidant benefits of green tea, to stimulate vitality and improve overall mood and well-being.

Ingredients:

- 1 tsp Ginseng root, finely sliced or grated

- 1 tbsp Green tea leaves

- 2 cups of hot water

- A dash of honey or lemon to taste

Instructions:

1. Mix ginseng and green tea in a teapot or infuser.

2. Pour hot water over the mixture and let steep for 3-5 minutes.

3. Strain into a cup, adding honey or lemon to enhance the flavor.

4. Drink in the morning or early afternoon to boost vitality and uplift your mood.

75. Ashwagandha & Hibiscus Stress Relief Tea

Intended Use: Utilizes the adaptogenic properties of ashwagandha to reduce stress and anxiety, complemented by the tangy flavor and mood-enhancing qualities of hibiscus, creating a tea that supports emotional balance and resilience.

Ingredients:

- 1 tsp Ashwagandha powder

- 1 tbsp dried Hibiscus flowers

- 2 cups of boiling water

- Honey to sweeten (optional)

Instructions:

1. Boil ashwagandha powder and hibiscus flowers in water for 10 minutes.

2. Strain the tea into a cup, sweetening with honey if desired.

3. Drink this tea in the evening or during times of high stress to promote a calm, positive mood and emotional well-being.

LIVER HEALTH

76. Dandelion & Milk Thistle Liver Cleanse Tea

Intended Use: Combines the detoxifying benefits of dandelion root with the liver-protective properties of milk thistle, creating a potent blend that supports liver function and helps cleanse toxins from the body.

Ingredients:

- 1 tbsp dried Dandelion root

- 1 tbsp dried Milk Thistle seeds

- 2 cups of boiling water

- Lemon wedge for added detoxification and flavor

Instructions:

1. Mix dandelion root and milk thistle seeds in a teapot or infuser.

2. Pour boiling water over the mixture and let steep for 15 minutes.

3. Strain into a cup and squeeze in the lemon wedge.

4. Drink this tea in the morning on an empty stomach to support liver detoxification and health.

77. Burdock Root & Chicory Liver Support Tea

Intended Use: Features burdock root for its blood purifying properties and chicory root for supporting liver metabolism, aiding in the digestion of fats and overall liver function.

Ingredients:

- 1 tbsp dried Burdock root

- 1 tbsp dried Chicory root

- 2.5 cups of water

- Honey to sweeten (optional)

Instructions:

1. Add burdock and chicory roots to a pot with water and bring to a boil.

2. Simmer for about 10 minutes, allowing the roots to release their beneficial properties.

3. Strain the tea into a mug, sweetening as desired.

4. Consume once daily to aid liver function and promote healthy digestion.

78. Turmeric & Ginger Liver Healing Tea

Intended Use: Utilizes the anti-inflammatory and antioxidant properties of turmeric alongside the warming effects of ginger, offering a healing and protective tea for liver health.

Ingredients:

- 1 tsp Turmeric powder (or 1 tbsp grated fresh turmeric root)
- 1 tsp fresh Ginger root, grated
- 2 cups of boiling water
- A pinch of black pepper (to enhance turmeric absorption)
- Lemon slice or honey to taste

Instructions:

1. Boil turmeric and ginger in water for 10 minutes.
2. Strain the tea into a cup, adding a pinch of black pepper to enhance curcumin absorption.
3. Add a slice of lemon or honey according to taste preference.
4. Drink regularly to support liver health and combat inflammation.

79. Peppermint & Lemon Balm Digestive Ease Tea

Intended Use: A soothing blend that combines peppermint and lemon balm, known for their digestive benefits, helping to ease liver stress by improving digestion and reducing bloating.

Ingredients:

- 1 tbsp dried Peppermint leaves
- 1 tbsp dried Lemon balm leaves
- 2 cups of boiling water
- A slice of fresh lemon (optional, for added digestive support and flavor)

Instructions:

1. Place peppermint and lemon balm in a tea infuser or pot.
2. Pour boiling water over the herbs and let steep for 10 minutes.
3. Strain and add a slice of fresh lemon if desired.
4. Drink after meals to aid digestion and support liver health.

80. Artichoke & Dandelion Bitter Boost Tea

Intended Use: Leverages the bitter compounds in artichoke and dandelion leaves, which stimulate bile production and support liver detoxification, enhancing overall liver function.

Ingredients:

- 1 tbsp dried Artichoke leaves
- 1 tbsp dried Dandelion leaves
- 2 cups of boiling water
- Honey or lemon to taste

Instructions:

1. Combine artichoke and dandelion leaves in a teapot or infuser.
2. Pour boiling water over and let steep for about 10-15 minutes.
3. Strain into a cup, adding honey or lemon to improve the bitter taste if needed.
4. Consume this tea regularly to stimulate liver function and promote detoxification.

KIDNEY SUPPORT

81. Nettle & Dandelion Diuretic Tea

Intended Use: Combines the cleansing and diuretic properties of stinging nettle with dandelion, creating a powerful blend that supports kidney function and helps flush toxins from the urinary tract.

Ingredients:

- 1 tbsp dried Stinging Nettle leaves

- 1 tbsp dried Dandelion leaves

- 2 cups of boiling water

- Lemon wedge or honey to taste

Instructions:

1. Mix nettle and dandelion leaves in a teapot or infuser.

2. Pour boiling water over the mixture and let steep for 10-15 minutes.

3. Strain into a cup, adding a squeeze of lemon or a bit of honey if desired.

4. Drink this tea daily to promote kidney health and support natural detoxification processes.

82. Parsley & Lemon Kidney Cleanse Tea

Intended Use: Utilizes parsley, known for its kidney-supporting nutrients and diuretic effect, and lemon for its detoxifying properties, offering a refreshing tea that helps cleanse the kidneys and stimulate urinary function.

Ingredients:

- A handful of fresh Parsley (or 1 tbsp dried Parsley)

- Juice of ½ a Lemon

- 2 cups of boiling water

- Honey (optional, for sweetness)

Instructions:

1. Place parsley in a teapot and cover with boiling water.

2. Let steep for about 10 minutes, then strain into a cup.

3. Stir in the fresh lemon juice, adding honey if you prefer a sweeter taste.

4. Consume once or twice a week to aid in kidney cleansing and enhance urinary tract health.

83. Cranberry & Hibiscus Urinary Tract Support Tea

Intended Use: A blend that combines the urinary tract health benefits of cranberries with the antioxidant properties of hibiscus, creating a tea that not only supports kidney function but also helps prevent urinary tract infections.

Ingredients:

- 1 tbsp dried Cranberries (or pure cranberry juice)
- 1 tbsp dried Hibiscus flowers
- 2 cups of boiling water
- Honey to sweeten (optional)

Instructions:

1. If using dried cranberries, crush them slightly before adding to a teapot along with hibiscus flowers.
2. Pour boiling water over the Ingredients and let steep for 10 minutes.
3. Strain into a cup and sweeten with honey as desired.
4. Drink regularly to maintain urinary tract health and support kidney function.

84. Horsetail & Corn Silk Mineral Support Tea

Intended Use: Features horsetail for its mineral content, particularly silica, which supports kidney and urinary tract health, and corn silk for its soothing and diuretic properties, aiding in the prevention of kidney stones and reducing inflammation.

Ingredients:

- 1 tbsp dried Horsetail
- 1 tbsp dried Corn Silk
- 2 cups of boiling water
- Lemon slice (optional, for flavor)

Instructions:

1. Combine horsetail and corn silk in a teapot or infuser.
2. Pour boiling water over the mixture and let steep for about 15 minutes.
3. Strain into a cup, adding a slice of lemon if desired.
4. Enjoy this tea 2-3 times a week to support kidney health and mineral balance.

85. Goldenrod & Birch Leaf Kidney Stone Prevention Tea

Intended Use: A preventive tea that uses goldenrod and birch leaves, known for their kidney support and stone-preventing properties. This blend helps increase urine flow and flush out toxins, potentially preventing the formation of kidney stones.

Ingredients:

- 1 tbsp dried Goldenrod
- 1 tbsp dried Birch leaves
- 2.5 cups of water
- Honey or lemon to taste

Instructions:

1. Add goldenrod and birch leaves to a pot of water and bring to a simmer.
2. Allow to simmer gently for about 10 minutes, then remove from heat and steep for an additional 5 minutes.
3. Strain the tea into a cup, adding honey or lemon to taste.
4. Consume occasionally as a preventive measure against kidney stones and to support overall kidney health.

MENSTRUAL SUPPORT

86. Raspberry Leaf & Ginger Menstrual Ease Tea

Intended Use: Combines the uterine toning properties of raspberry leaf with the warming and anti-inflammatory effects of ginger, creating a soothing blend that helps alleviate menstrual cramps and discomfort.

Ingredients:

- 1 tbsp dried Raspberry leaf
- 1 tsp fresh Ginger root, grated
- 2 cups of boiling water
- Honey to taste (optional)

Instructions:

1. Place raspberry leaf and grated ginger in a teapot or infuser.
2. Pour boiling water over the mixture and let steep for 10-15 minutes.
3. Strain into a cup and sweeten with honey if desired.
4. Drink a cup 1-2 times daily during menstruation to ease cramps and discomfort.

87. Chamomile & Peppermint Bloating Relief Tea

Intended Use: Utilizes the calming properties of chamomile and the digestive benefits of peppermint to relieve menstrual bloating and digestive issues, promoting a sense of comfort and well-being.

Ingredients:

- 1 tbsp dried Chamomile flowers
- 1 tbsp dried Peppermint leaves
- 2 cups of boiling water
- Lemon slice (optional, for added flavor and vitamin C)

Instructions:

1. Mix chamomile and peppermint leaves in a teapot or infuser.
2. Pour boiling water over the herbs and let steep for 5-7 minutes.
3. Strain and add a slice of lemon if desired.
4. Drink as needed to reduce bloating and soothe menstrual discomfort.

88. Nettle & Dandelion Iron Boost Tea

Intended Use: A nutrient-rich tea that combines nettle and dandelion, both known for their high mineral content, including iron, which is often needed in greater amounts during menstruation due to blood loss.

Ingredients:

- 1 tbsp dried Nettle leaves
- 1 tbsp dried Dandelion leaves
- 2.5 cups of water
- Honey or lemon to taste

Instructions:

1. Add nettle and dandelion leaves to a pot of water and bring to a boil.
2. Simmer for about 10 minutes to extract the minerals.
3. Strain the tea into a cup, adding honey or lemon to taste.
4. Drink daily, especially during menstruation, to support iron levels and overall vitality.

89. Cinnamon & Clove Hormonal Balance Tea

Intended Use: Features cinnamon and clove, both of which have warming properties and can help regulate menstrual cycles and balance hormones, providing relief from menstrual irregularities and symptoms of PMS.

Ingredients:

- 1 tsp ground Cinnamon
- 3-4 whole Cloves
- 2 cups of boiling water
- Honey to sweeten (optional)

Instructions:

1. Add cinnamon and cloves to boiling water and simmer for 5 minutes.
2. Remove from heat and let steep for an additional 10 minutes.
3. Strain into a mug, sweetening as desired.
4. Enjoy this tea in the week leading up to menstruation to help balance hormones and regulate cycles.

90. Lemon Balm & Licorice Mood Support Tea

Intended Use: A comforting blend that uses lemon balm for its mood-enhancing properties and licorice root for its ability to support adrenal health, reducing stress and elevating mood during menstruation.

Ingredients:

- 1 tbsp dried Lemon balm leaves

- 1 tsp Licorice root, chopped

- 2 cups of boiling water

- A slice of fresh ginger (optional, for added warmth and digestion support)

Instructions:

1. Combine lemon balm, licorice root, and ginger (if using) in a teapot or infuser.

2. Pour boiling water over the mixture and let steep for 10-15 minutes.

3. Strain into a cup and enjoy as needed for mood support and stress relief during your menstrual cycle.

ANTIOXIDANT BOOST

91. Green Tea & Hibiscus Antioxidant Fusion

Intended Use: A potent combination of antioxidant-rich green tea and hibiscus, this tea blend offers a delicious way to fight free radicals and support cardiovascular health.

Ingredients:

- 1 tbsp Green tea leaves

- 1 tbsp dried Hibiscus flowers

- 2 cups of boiling water

- Honey or lemon to taste

Instructions:

1. Place green tea leaves and hibiscus flowers in a teapot or infuser.

2. Pour boiling water over the mixture and let steep for 5 minutes.

3. Strain into a cup, adding honey or lemon according to preference.

4. Drink daily to enjoy the antioxidant benefits and support overall well-being.

92. Turmeric & Ginger Golden Antioxidant Tea

Intended Use: Combining the anti-inflammatory powers of turmeric with the digestive benefits of ginger, this warming tea is perfect for enhancing immunity and providing a strong antioxidant boost.

Ingredients:

- 1 tsp Turmeric powder (or 1 tbsp grated fresh turmeric root)

- 1 tsp fresh Ginger root, grated

- 2 cups of boiling water

- A pinch of black pepper (to enhance turmeric absorption)

- Honey to taste

Instructions:

1. Boil turmeric and ginger in water for 10 minutes.

2. Strain the tea into a cup, adding a pinch of black pepper to enhance absorption of turmeric's active compound, curcumin.

3. Sweeten with honey if desired.

4. Enjoy this vibrant tea regularly to boost antioxidant intake and reduce inflammation.

93. Rosehip & Elderberry Immune Boosting Tea

Intended Use: A nutrient-dense tea that harnesses the high vitamin C content of rosehips and the immune-boosting properties of elderberries, ideal for cold and flu season.

Ingredients:

- 1 tbsp dried Rosehips

- 1 tbsp dried Elderberries

- 2.5 cups of water

- Honey to sweeten (optional)

Instructions:

1. Add rosehips and elderberries to a pot of water and bring to a boil.

2. Simmer for about 15 minutes to extract their full benefits.

3. Strain the tea into a mug, sweetening as desired.

4. Drink during the colder months or whenever you need an immune and antioxidant boost.

94. Matcha & Lemon Vitality Tea

Intended Use: Utilizing the whole-leaf benefits of matcha green tea powder, this tea provides a powerful dose of antioxidants, enhanced with a touch of lemon for detoxifying benefits and vitamin C.

Ingredients:

- 1 tsp Matcha green tea powder

- 2 cups of hot water (not boiling)

- Juice of ½ a lemon

- Honey to taste (optional)

Instructions:

1. Whisk matcha powder in hot water until fully dissolved.

2. Stir in the lemon juice, adding honey to sweeten if desired.

3. Enjoy this energizing tea in the morning or before exercise to benefit from its high antioxidant content and vitality-boosting properties.

95. Cinnamon & Clove Spice Antioxidant Tea

Intended Use: A warming spice tea that combines the antioxidant power of cinnamon and cloves, offering a delightful way to improve blood sugar regulation and support digestive health.

Ingredients:

- 1 tsp ground Cinnamon

- 3-4 whole Cloves

- 2 cups of boiling water

- A slice of orange (optional, for added flavor and antioxidants)

Instructions:

1. Add cinnamon and cloves to boiling water and simmer for 5 minutes.

2. Remove from heat and let steep for an additional 10 minutes.

3. Strain into a mug, adding a slice of orange if desired for enhanced flavor and extra antioxidant benefits.

4. Sip in the evening to unwind or after meals to aid digestion and enjoy the spices' antioxidant properties.

COLD AND FLU RELIEF

96. Echinacea & Elderberry Immune Support Tea

Intended Use: A powerful blend combining echinacea, known for its immune-enhancing properties, with elderberries, recognized for their antiviral effects, making this tea ideal for cold and flu prevention and recovery.

Ingredients:

- 1 tbsp dried Echinacea

- 1 tbsp dried Elderberries

- 2.5 cups of water

- Honey or lemon to taste

Instructions:

1. Add echinacea and elderberries to a pot of water and bring to a simmer.

2. Simmer gently for 15 minutes to extract the herbs' full benefits.

3. Strain the tea into a mug, sweetening with honey or adding lemon to taste.

4. Drink 2-3 times daily at the first sign of cold or flu symptoms to support the immune system.

97. Ginger & Honey Soothing Tea

Intended Use: Utilizes the warming and anti-inflammatory properties of ginger, combined with the soothing and antibacterial effects of honey, to relieve sore throats and calm coughs.

Ingredients:

- 1 tsp fresh Ginger root, grated

- 2 cups of boiling water

- 1 tbsp Honey (preferably raw)

- Juice of ½ a lemon (optional, for added vitamin C and flavor)

Instructions:

1. Steep grated ginger in boiling water for 10 minutes.

2. Strain the tea into a mug, stirring in honey and lemon juice if using.

3. Drink warm, especially in the morning or before bed, to soothe the throat and alleviate coughing.

98. Thyme & Licorice Root Cough Tea

Intended Use: A therapeutic blend that combines thyme, with its expectorant properties, and licorice root, which soothes the throat and eases coughs, providing relief for persistent coughing associated with colds and flu.

Ingredients:

- 1 tbsp dried Thyme leaves
- 1 tsp Licorice root, chopped
- 2 cups of boiling water
- A slice of lemon or a dash of cinnamon (optional, for flavor)

Instructions:

1. Mix thyme and licorice root in a teapot or infuser.
2. Pour boiling water over the mixture and let steep for 10-15 minutes.
3. Strain into a cup, adding lemon or cinnamon as desired.
4. Consume as needed to manage cough and soothe the respiratory tract.

99. Peppermint & Eucalyptus Congestion Relief Tea

Intended Use: Combines the decongestant properties of peppermint and eucalyptus, offering a refreshing tea that helps clear nasal congestion and relieve headaches associated with colds and flu.

Ingredients:

- 1 tbsp dried Peppermint leaves
- 1 tsp dried Eucalyptus leaves
- 2 cups of boiling water
- Honey to taste (optional)

Instructions:

1. Place peppermint and eucalyptus leaves in a tea infuser or pot.
2. Pour boiling water over the herbs and let steep for 10 minutes.
3. Strain and sweeten with honey if desired.
4. Drink hot to help relieve congestion and sinus pressure.

100. Lemon Balm & Chamomile Fever Reducer Tea

Intended Use: A gentle, calming tea using lemon balm and chamomile, both known for their fever-reducing and relaxing effects, making this blend perfect for restful sleep during cold and flu recovery.

Ingredients:

- 1 tbsp dried Lemon balm leaves

- 1 tbsp dried Chamomile flowers

- 2 cups of boiling water

- Honey or lemon to taste

Instructions:

1. Combine lemon balm and chamomile in a teapot or infuser.

2. Pour boiling water over and let steep for 5-7 minutes.

3. Strain into a cup, adding honey or lemon according to preference.

4. Drink before bedtime to help reduce fever and promote a restful night's sleep during illness.

TOP FAVORITES

101. Energizing Morning Blend

Intended Use: This tea is designed to invigorate your morning routine without the jitters associated with coffee. By blending the stimulating properties of green tea with the adaptogenic benefits of ginseng and the refreshing touch of peppermint, this tea provides a balanced energy boost. It's perfect for those seeking a natural way to kickstart their day, enhancing mental alertness and physical stamina.

Ingredients:

- 1 tbsp dried Green Tea leaves

- 1 tsp dried Ginseng root

- 1 tsp Peppermint leaves

- Honey or lemon to taste

Instructions:

1. Combine green tea, ginseng, and peppermint in a teapot.

2. Pour 2 cups of hot water (not boiling) over the herbs and let steep for 3-5 minutes.

3. Strain into a mug, adding honey or lemon according to preference.

4. Savor this blend in the morning to energize your day naturally.

102. Gut Soothing Digestive Tea

Intended Use: Crafted for those experiencing digestive discomfort, this tea combines fennel, chamomile, and ginger—herbs known for their soothing digestive properties. The blend aims to ease bloating, support digestion, and calm the digestive tract, making it an ideal after-meal companion for individuals seeking natural digestive aid.

Ingredients:

- 1 tbsp dried Fennel seeds

- 1 tbsp dried Chamomile flowers

- 1 tsp Ginger root, grated

- Optional: A pinch of licorice root for sweetness

Instructions:

1. Lightly crush the fennel seeds to release their oils.

2. Combine fennel, chamomile, and ginger in a teapot.

3. Pour 2 cups of boiling water over the mixture and let steep for 10 minutes.

4. Strain and serve warm. Sweeten with licorice root if desired.

5. Enjoy after meals to aid digestion and soothe the digestive system.

103. Skin Radiance Herbal Tea

Intended Use: This tea is a blend of nettle, red clover, and calendula, selected for their skin-supporting properties. Rich in nutrients and antioxidants, it aims to purify the blood and support skin health from within, promoting clarity and a natural glow. Ideal for individuals looking to enhance their skin's health naturally.

Ingredients:

- 1 tbsp dried Nettle leaves

- 1 tbsp dried Red Clover flowers

- 1 tsp dried Calendula petals

- Lemon slice or honey to taste

Instructions:

1. Blend nettle, red clover, and calendula in a teapot.

2. Add 2 cups of boiling water and steep for 15 minutes to extract the full spectrum of benefits.

3. Strain into a cup and add a slice of lemon or a dollop of honey for flavor.

4. Drink regularly to support skin health from within.

104. Heart Harmony Tea

Intended Use: This tea blends hibiscus and hawthorn berries, known for their heart-protective properties, with rosehips to enhance the blend's vitamin C content. It's crafted to support cardiovascular health, lower blood pressure, and provide a rich source of antioxidants. A perfect daily tea for those focusing on nurturing their heart health.

Ingredients:

- 1 tbsp Hibiscus flowers

- 1 tbsp Hawthorn berries

- 1 tsp Rosehips

- Optional: Honey for natural sweetness

Instructions:

1. Combine hibiscus, hawthorn berries, and rosehips in a teapot.

2. Pour 2 cups of boiling water over the herbs and let steep for 10 minutes.

3. Strain into a mug, adding honey if a sweeter taste is desired.

4. Consume this tea daily for heart health and antioxidant support.

105. Soothing Cold Relief Tea

Intended Use: This blend is specifically formulated with echinacea and elderflower, both celebrated for their immune-boosting effects, along with lemon balm to ease stress and enhance relaxation during illness. The addition of lemon juice not only adds a refreshing flavor but also boosts the vitamin C content, supporting the body's immune response against cold and flu symptoms.

Ingredients:

- 1 tbsp dried Echinacea

- 1 tbsp dried Elderflower

- 1 tsp Lemon Balm leaves

- Juice of ½ a lemon

Instructions:

1. Place echinacea, elderflower, and lemon balm in a teapot.

2. Pour 2 cups of boiling water over the herbs and steep for 10-15 minutes.

3. Strain the tea into a mug and stir in the fresh lemon juice.

4. Sip slowly to enjoy the immune-boosting effects and alleviate cold symptoms.

CONCLUSION

As we reach the end of this herbal tea odyssey, it's clear that what began as a simple exploration of tea has blossomed into a profound journey of discovery, wellness, and connection. Inspired by Barbara O'Neill's wisdom, we've traversed the globe, delved into ancient traditions, and unlocked the secrets of nature's pharmacy, all through the humble act of brewing tea. This cookbook has not just shared recipes; it has opened a door to a world where health is nurtured naturally, where each sip of tea is a communion with the earth, and where the rituals of preparation and consumption are acts of self-care and reverence for life. We've learned that tea is more than a beverage—it's a medium for healing, a catalyst for change, and a companion on the path to wellness.

By crafting your herbal tea remedies, you're not just brewing beverages; you're weaving a tapestry of health that spans the physical, emotional, and spiritual. You're embracing a practice that is as ancient as it is timely, joining a community of healers, herbalists, and health seekers who understand that true wellness begins with what we choose to put into our bodies and how we choose to live our lives. As you continue on your tea journey, let this cookbook be your guide and companion. Experiment with blends, listen to your body, and find joy in the process. Remember, the path to wellness is personal and unique, filled with discovery, growth, and the occasional surprise. Thank you for embarking on this journey with us. May your cup always be full, your heart always light, and your health ever flourishing. Here's to many more cups of tea, moments of tranquility, and steps towards a healthier, happier life.

Made in the USA
Las Vegas, NV
20 July 2024

92579190R00046